THE
TOTALLY
P...
C...

THE
TOTALLY
POTATO
COOKBOOK

By Helene Siegel & Karen Gillingham
Illustrated by Carolyn Vibbert

CELESTIAL ARTS
BERKELEY, CALIFORNIA

The Totally Potato Cookbook is produced by becker&mayer!, Ltd.
Kirkland, Washington.
www.beckermayer.com

Printed in Singapore.

Cover design and illustration: Bob Greisen
Interior design: Susan Hernday
Interior illustrations: Carolyn Vibbert
Typesetting: Matt Hutnak

Library of Congress Cataloging-in-Publication Data

Siegel, Helene
    The totally potatoes cookbook/by Helene Siegel and Karen Gillingham.
        p. cm.
    ISBN 0-89087-947-8 (pbk.)
    1. Cookery (Potatoes) 2. Potatoes. I. Gillingham, Karen. II Title.

TX803.p8 S54 2000
641.6'521--dc21

                                                                99-052659

Celestial Arts Publishing
P.O. Box 7123
Berkeley, CA 94707

Look for all 32 *Totally* books at your local store!

To our Moms

CONTENTS

INTRODUCTION

Potatoes are easy. All they ask for is fat and salt to make the transition from homely spud to addictive food thing: think snappy potato chips; matchstick thin, well-salted french fries; and tender-on-the-inside, browned-on-the-outside potato pancakes.

For those who need more motivation to get to know America's most popular vegetable better, let's not forget how handy a potato is in the kitchen. It can add heft and earthy character to stews, vegetable soups, and meat pies, can be mashed into delectable dumplings, and can even be the secret ingredient in a special chocolate cake.

Potatoes are inexpensive, available year-round, easily stored, and supremely versatile. They can be mashed, roasted, fried, baked, gratinéed, boiled, steamed, and grilled. They offset rich, spicy foods with their comforting blandness, and yet, once fried, they're the perfect crisp accompaniment to roasted and grilled meats and fish, barbecued burgers, and roasted chicken.

You can never have too many recipes for potatoes. So whether you're looking to shore up your spud intelligence with basics such as the very best mashed, baked, or fried; or you're wondering what to do with those adorable new fingerlings you've spied at the farmers market; or you need some fresh new salad ideas for this season's cookout, the answer lies within. Dig in and enjoy!

How to Choose and Store Potatoes

Shop for firm, unwrinkled potatoes, and store in a cool, dark place—not the refrigerator. Chilling turns the potato's starch to sugar, and sunlight develops solanine—the alkaloid that turns them green. Any green patches of skin, eyes, or sprouts should be removed before cooking since they may be toxic.

POTATO
TIDBITS

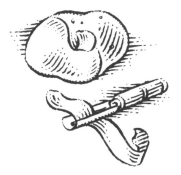

HOMEMADE POTATO CHIPS

If you think packaged potato chips are addicting, wait until you start crunching on these deliciously crisp slivers.

1 pound baking or sweet potatoes
peanut or vegetable oil for deep-frying
salt

Peel potatoes, if desired. Trim one end of each potato to make a flat surface. Using a vegetable peeler, the thinnest slicing blade of a food processor, or a mandoline, slice potatoes, starting at flat end, as thinly as possible. Place in a large bowl of ice water.

In a deep fryer, wok, Dutch oven, or a heavy, deep skillet set over a medium-high burner, heat 2 to 4 inches oil to 375 degrees F.

Drain potato slices, and blot dry. Without crowding pan, fry 10 to 20 at a time, just until golden for baking potatoes or deep brown for sweet potatoes. With skimmer or slotted spoon, transfer chips to paper towels to drain. Sprinkle with salt to taste.

To prepare in advance, do not salt after frying, and store in airtight container. Reheat in a 375-degree oven, pat off oil with paper towels, add salt, and serve.

MAKES ABOUT 6 CUPS

FINGER POTATOES
WITH CAVIAR

Here's an elegant appetizer for champagne occasions.

12 small red or yellow Finn potatoes
coarse salt
1 cup (8-ounces) sour cream
4 ounces caviar or salmon roe

Bring a large pot of salted water to a boil. Add the potatoes and cook 15 to 20 minutes, until they can be pierced with a fork but the skins remain intact. Be careful not to overcook. Drain, rinse with cold water, and drain again. Pat dry with towels.

Halve the potatoes lengthwise. Using a melon baller or a small spoon, scoop out a cavity in each center. If making in advance, arrange on a platter, cover, and refrigerate until serving time.

To serve, fill each potato half with a dollop of sour cream and then top cream with a small spoonful of caviar or salmon eggs. (Use separate spoons for the cream and eggs, to prevent the colors from blending.) Serve immediately or reserve in the refrigerator.

MAKES 24 PIECES

ROASTED SCALLOPS
ON POTATO DISKS

Buttery Yukon golds are a good foil for the richness of luscious sea scallops.

2 Yukon gold potatoes
¼ cup olive oil
salt and pepper
8 large sea scallops, about 1 pound
4 garlic cloves, thinly sliced lengthwise
2 plum tomatoes, seeded and roughly
    chopped
1 tablespoon chopped fresh rosemary
¼ teaspoon crushed red pepper flakes
8 lemon wedges

Preheat oven to 450 degrees F.

Cut potatoes into ½-inch-thick disks to yield 8 slices. Brush with olive oil and arrange in a single layer on baking sheet. Sprinkle with salt and pepper to taste. Roast 20 minutes, turning halfway.

In a shallow casserole, arrange scallops in a single layer. Scatter garlic, tomatoes, rosemary, and red pepper flakes over scallops. Season to taste with salt and pepper. Drizzle with remaining olive oil. Place in oven with potatoes for last 10 minutes of roasting time.

To serve, place potato disks on a platter or individual serving dishes. Top each disk with a scallop, and spoon tomato mixture from pan over top. Garnish with lemon wedges.

SERVES 4

POTATO PANCAKE WITH SMOKED SALMON

We love the contrast between crisp, flat potato pancakes and silky smoked salmon.

1 "Two Potato Pancake" (see page 59)
¼ pound thinly sliced smoked salmon
2 tablespoons sour cream

Make the potato pancake according to directions. To serve, cut the pancake into 6 wedges, and top each with a thin slice of salmon. Dot with a teaspoonful of sour cream. Serve warm.

SERVES 6

EARTHY SALADS
AND SOUPS

SUMMER PISTOU SOUP

Feel free to improvise with your favorite vegetables in this traditional French soup. Just cook all the root vegetables and potatoes before adding the softer, quicker cooking vegetables. And don't leave out the rustic pesto-and-bread garnish. It makes it sing.

3 small red potatoes, with skins
1 large carrot, peeled
1 medium onion
2 small zucchini or yellow squash
1 celery stalk
2 large tomatoes, seeded and chopped
8 cups chicken stock
salt and freshly ground pepper to taste
1 baguette, cut in ½-inch slices and crisply
  toasted
½ cup prepared pesto
grated Parmesan for sprinkling

Cut all the vegetables into ½-inch dice.

Bring chicken stock to a boil in a large stockpot. Add potatoes, carrot, and onion and return to a boil. Reduce to a simmer, and cook uncovered, 20 minutes. Add squash, celery, and tomatoes. Return to a boil, reduce heat to a simmer, and cook 15 minutes longer. Season to taste with salt and pepper.

Spread the pesto on the toasted bread slices. Place 1 slice on the bottom of each soup bowl, and ladle hot soup on top. Serve with remaining pesto and add Parmesan to taste.

SERVES 4 TO 6

"What I have tried to do is convey the idea that those people, eating their potatoes by lamplight, have dug the earth with the very hands they put into their bowls."

—Vincent Van Gogh on his painting
"The Potato Eaters"

POTATO POBLANO SOUP

A smooth, velvety potato soup such as this one looks lovely served with a dollop of tomato salsa or roasted red pepper purée in the center for color.

3 tablespoons butter
3 garlic cloves, minced
1 medium onion, chopped
2 poblano chiles, roasted, peeled, seeded, and
    chopped
1 teaspoon ground cumin
salt and freshly ground pepper, to taste
4 cups chicken stock
2 pounds boiling potatoes, chopped, with
    skins
1 cup milk

Melt the butter in a large stockpot over medium-high heat. Sauté garlic, onion, poblanos, cumin, salt, and pepper until onions are soft, about 7 minutes.

Pour in chicken stock and potatoes. Bring to a boil, reduce to a simmer, and cook uncovered, until potatoes are done, about 30 minutes. Transfer to a food processor or blender, and purée until smooth.

Pour back into stockpot, add milk, and bring back to a boil. Serve hot.

SERVES 4

Nutritional Value
A plain, medium-size potato contains about 100 calories and is high in vitamin C, potassium, and fiber. Potatoes contain no fat, cholesterol, or sodium. The problem with potatoes lies in the company they keep. Butter, sour cream, and oil are to blame for the plain potato's rich reputation.

ROASTED RED POTATO SALAD

We're totally hooked on roasted potato salads because they deliver so much flavor with so little fat.

2 pounds small red potatoes
¼ cup extra virgin olive oil
2 sprigs fresh rosemary
salt and freshly ground pepper
4 scallions, white and light green parts,
    chopped
1 teaspoon Dijon mustard
2 tablespoons red wine vinegar

Preheat oven to 425 degrees F.

In a medium roasting pan or ovenproof casserole, toss the potatoes with 2 tablespoons of the olive oil, rosemary, and plenty of salt and pepper. Roast uncovered, stirring occasionally, until the potatoes are tender, about 45 minutes. Cool slightly.

In a large bowl, combine scallions, mustard, red wine vinegar, and remaining 2 tablespoons olive oil. Season with salt and pepper. Whisk together to form a vinaigrette. When cool enough to handle, cut potatoes in half. Add to bowl with vinaigrette and toss to coat evenly. Season to taste with salt and pepper, and serve warm or at room temperature.

SERVES 4

PROVENÇAL VEGETABLE SALAD

Our inspiration for this garlicky composed salad is the classic Niçoise salad minus the tuna.

1 pound small red potatoes, cut in chunks
½ pound green beans, trimmed and cut into
    1-inch lengths
3 large garlic cloves, unpeeled
olive oil for sprinkling
salt
3 anchovy fillets
juice of 2 lemons
½ cup extra virgin olive oil
freshly ground pepper
Tabasco
2 plum tomatoes, cut in 4 wedges each
2 hard-cooked eggs, peeled and quartered
½ cup Niçoise or Kalamata olives

Preheat oven to 400 degrees F.

Arrange the potatoes, green beans, and garlic in a single layer in a roasting pan. Drizzle with olive oil, sprinkle with salt, and bake until potatoes are tender, about 40 minutes. Remove garlic with a slotted spoon, and cool slightly.

Squeeze garlic cloves to peel, and place pulp in a blender. Add anchovies, lemon juice, olive oil, black pepper, to taste, and a few dashes Tabasco. Blend to form a dressing.

In the center of a serving platter, heap drained, warm potatoes and beans. In piles around the rim of the plate, arrange tomato, egg wedges, and olives. Spoon the garlic dressing over all, reserving any leftover dressing in the refrigerator.

SERVES 2 (AS A MAIN COURSE)

COLD VINAIGRETTE POTATO SALAD

A layer of these crisp, cold, thinly sliced potatoes is terrific served under a fillet of grilled or roasted fish.

6 medium red potatoes, with skins, very thinly sliced and rinsed in cold water
½ large red onion, thinly sliced
¼ cup lemon juice
1 tablespoon Dijon mustard
4 garlic cloves, minced
¼ cup olive oil
¼ cup chopped fresh oregano or Italian parsley leaves
salt and freshly ground pepper

Cook the potatoes in a large pot of rapidly boiling salted water 2 minutes, once the water begins to boil. Drain in a colander, and transfer to a large mixing bowl. Add the red onion, and toss.

In a small bowl, whisk together the remaining ingredients to form a vinaigrette. Pour over the potatoes and onions, toss well, and season to taste with salt and pepper. Serve or store in the refrigerator for up to 5 days.

SERVES 8

"Some potato salads are sublime, some are miraculous, and some are merely ordinary, but I have yet to taste any that was awful."
— *Laurie Colwin in* Home Cooking

GERMAN POTATO SALAD

This is the classic accompaniment to hot dogs and burgers for summer barbecues.

2½ pounds boiling potatoes
6 scallions, chopped
½ cup chicken broth
2 tablespoons olive oil
1 tablespoon cider vinegar
½ teaspoon dry mustard
¼ teaspoon celery seed
salt and pepper
½ cup sour cream or yogurt
4 bacon slices, crisp fried and crumbled
2 tablespoons chopped fresh dill

Cook potatoes in boiling salted water to cover until tender, about 20 minutes. Drain. While still warm, peel, if desired, and cut into 1-inch cubes. Set aside in a bowl, and keep warm.

In a saucepan, combine scallions, broth, oil, vinegar, mustard, celery seed, and salt and pepper to taste. Bring to a simmer, and cook for 2 minutes. Cool slightly, then stir in sour cream. Pour dressing over warm potatoes, and mix well. Sprinkle with bacon and dill.

SERVES 6

"Found a little patched-up inn in the village of Bulson....Proprietor had nothing but potatoes; but what a feast he laid before me. Served them in five different courses—potato soup, potato fricassee, potatoes creamed, potato salad, and finished with potato pie. It may be because I had not eaten in thirty-six hours, but that meal seems about the best I ever had."
—*General Douglas MacArthur*

Know Your Spuds

- *The russet Burbank, also know as the Idaho, is a large, brown-skinned, white-fleshed potato. Because of its high starch, low water content, it is ideal for baking, mashing, and frying.*

- *Round red or white potatoes, are medium-size, medium-starch potatoes with thin skin and waxy flesh. These all-purpose potatoes are good for boiling, steaming, and roasting. Since they hold their shape, they are great for salads.*

- *The term "new potatoes" refers to small, hard, immature low-starch potatoes. With their thinner, more digestible skins, they are delicious boiled, steamed, or roasted and eaten in their skins.*

- *Yukon gold and yellow Finn are two yellow-fleshed varieties now available in most markets. Their rich, creamy flesh tastes buttery, and they are terrific boiled, roasted, or mashed.*

- *Sweet potatoes have light tan skin and yellow flesh. They bake up dry and flaky like a potato. Darker-skinned "yams" (a misnomer since they are not yams at all) have orange flesh and a moister, sweeter flavor.*

POTATO DINNERS

POTATO TORTILLA

This simple combination of eggs and potatoes is amazingly satisfying.

¼ cup olive oil
2 large baking potatoes, peeled and thinly
   sliced
salt and freshly ground pepper
2 garlic cloves, minced
1 large onion, thinly sliced
6 eggs

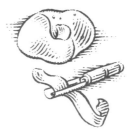

Heat ¼ cup of the oil in a 9-inch cast-iron skillet over high heat. Fry the potatoes, turning occasionally, until golden and crisp, about 15 minutes. Drain on paper towels, and wipe pan clean.

In another skillet, heat 2 tablespoons of the oil over medium-low heat. Sauté the garlic and onion, until soft and golden. Remove from heat.

Preheat oven to 350 degrees F.

In a large bowl, beat the eggs. Stir in the cooked potatoes and the onion mixture. Heat the remaining oil in the potato skillet over low heat. Pour in the egg mixture, smoothing the top. Cook until the bottom is golden, then invert onto a plate. Slide the tortilla back into the pan, crisp-side up. Transfer to oven, and bake until the edges are set, about 5 minutes. Cool in the pan, and cut into wedges to serve.

SERVES 6 TO 12

HACHIS PARMENTIER

This cozy mashed potato pie stuffed with ground meat is named for Auguste Parmentier, the man who popularized the potato in France.

2 pounds baking potatoes, peeled and cut in chunks
2 tablespoons vegetable oil
6 tablespoons butter
4 garlic cloves, minced
1 medium onion, diced
1½ pounds chopped sirloin
salt and freshly ground pepper
1 cup milk
¼ cup chopped fresh parsley
¼ cup grated Parmesan or Gruyère cheese

Place the potatoes in a medium saucepan with enough water to cover. Boil until soft, about 20 minutes.

Preheat the oven to 350 degrees F.

Heat the oil and 1 tablespoon of the butter in a large skillet over medium heat. Sauté the garlic and onion until soft. Add the meat, salt, and pepper to taste, and fry over high heat, stirring and breaking up with a spoon, until evenly browned.

Melt 3 tablespoons of the butter with milk in a small saucepan over low heat. Drain the potatoes, leaving them in their pan, and slowly pour in the hot milk mixture, mixing and mashing until smooth. Season with salt and pepper.

Coat a 9-inch pie pan with butter. Spread half of the mashed potatoes in the pan. Using a slotted spoon to drain the meat, spread it over the potatoes in the pan, and then sprinkle with parsley. Top with the remaining potatoes, sprinkle with cheese, and dot with the remaining butter. Bake uncovered 40 minutes, until the top is crusty and brown.

SERVES 4

SHEPHERD'S PIE

No pie crust is necessary for this rib-sticking winter meal of browned meat, veggies, and mashed potatoes.

1 medium onion, peeled and chopped
1 green bell pepper, roughly chopped
2 carrots, roughly chopped
2 tablespoons vegetable oil
1½ pounds ground beef or lamb
1 beef bouillon cube, dissolved in ½ cup
    boiling water
1 tablespoon cornstarch mixed with
    2 tablespoons water
1 tablespoon Worcestershire sauce
Salt and pepper
3 cups hot "Classic Mashed Potatoes" (see
    page 68)
2 tablespoons butter

Preheat oven to 400 degrees F.

In a large skillet over medium heat, sauté onion, green pepper, and carrots in oil until onion is golden, about 10 minutes. Add beef, and cook, breaking up meat with spoon, until lightly browned, about 10 minutes. Drain and discard fat.

Stir beef bouillon, cornstarch mixture, and Worcestershire into meat mixture. Cook over low heat, stirring frequently, for 2 minutes. Season to taste with salt and pepper. Transfer mixture to buttered 1½-quart casserole. Spread potatoes over top. Bake 25 minutes. Dot with butter, then cook under broiler until browned, about 2 minutes.

SERVES 4 TO 6

RIGATONI WITH POTATOES AND SWISS CHARD

This rustic dish of pasta and potatoes balanced with tart chard should satisfy any carbohydrate cravings for a while. Meat eaters may want to sauté three-quarters to one pound of crumbled Italian sausage along with the garlic.

1 large baking potato (about ¾ pound), peeled and cut into 1-inch cubes
1 bunch Swiss chard, stems removed, leaves cut in strips
1 pound rigatoni
¼ cup olive oil, or more
2 garlic cloves, roughly chopped
¼ teaspoon red pepper flakes
salt and pepper
grated Parmesan cheese

Bring a large pot of salted water to a boil. Add potato and chard. When water returns to a boil, add rigatoni and continue to cook until pasta is al dente, about 10 minutes.

Meanwhile, heat olive oil in a large saucepan over medium heat. Sauté garlic just until golden, about 1 minute. Add red pepper flakes. Remove from heat.

Drain pasta and vegetables, and add to garlic mixture in pan. Toss to mix thoroughly. Season to taste with salt, pepper, and red pepper flakes, and transfer to a serving bowl.

SERVES 4

"Blessed by stubborn and powerful instinct [potato plants] push aside soil to make room for themselves; they grow and grow, filling themselves with what later will be our digestible, sour-cream-topped, buttery joy."
—Judith Moore in Never Eat Your Heart Out

POTATO, ONION, AND GORGONZOLA PIZZA

The idea of potato on a pizza may seem odd, but once you taste it we think you'll agree it's a winner!

1 large boiling potato, about ½ pound, peeled and very thinly sliced
½ small onion, thinly sliced
1 (1-pound) loaf defrosted white bread dough, or 1 large prebaked Boboli crust
1 cup shredded mozzarella cheese
salt and pepper
¾ cup crumbled Gorgonzola cheese
3 small sprigs fresh rosemary

Preheat oven to 450 degrees F.

Cook potato and onion in boiling salted water to cover for 2 minutes. Drain and set aside.

Roll out bread dough to 12- to 14-inch circle, and place on pizza pan or baking sheet, or place Boboli crust on sheet. Scatter mozzarella evenly over dough, leaving 1 inch bare around the rim for a crust. Top with potato and onions. Sprinkle with salt and pepper to taste. Scatter with Gorgonzola, then top with rosemary. Bake until crust is deep golden and cheese is bubbly, about 10 minutes.

SERVES 2 TO 3

POTATO GNOCCHI

Gnocchi are tiny, light potato dumplings eaten like pasta in Italy.

2 cups hot mashed baking potatoes
1 cup all-purpose flour, plus more for
    kneading
1 teaspoon salt
2 teaspoons olive oil
1 egg, lightly beaten
2 tablespoons melted butter

In a large bowl, combine potatoes, flour, salt, and oil. Mix with a fork. Add egg, and mix well. Turn dough out onto floured surface and knead about 15 turns, working in more flour if dough is too soft. Gather into a ball, and set on floured surface.

Break off about ½-cup portions of dough at a time and roll each into a ½-inch-thick rope. Cut rope into 1¼-inch lengths. Place finger in center of each length, and wrap the dough into a bow shape, arranging them on a floured baking sheet.

Preheat oven to 180 degrees F. Place butter in a shallow-rimmed ovenproof dish.

Bring a large pot of salted water to a boil. Add gnocchi, about 2 dozen at a time, to boiling water. After they rise to the surface, cook 5 minutes. With a slotted spoon, transfer to a prepared pan, turning gnocchi to coat with butter. Keep warm in oven until all are cooked. Serve with "Roasted Red Pepper Sauce" (see page 46) or your favorite tomato sauce.

SERVES 4

ROASTED RED PEPPER SAUCE FOR POTATO GNOCCHI

Gnocchi are also delicious with seasoned butter or thickened cream.

3 red bell peppers
2 garlic cloves
¼ cup olive oil
salt and pepper
2 tablespoons chopped Italian parsley
"Potato Gnocchi" (see page 44)

Preheat oven to 350 degrees F.

Arrange peppers on baking sheet. Roast, turning occasionally, until blistered all over, about 25 minutes. When cool enough to handle, peel, stem, and seed the peppers. In a food processor or blender, combine the peppers, garlic, and olive oil. Process until puréed. Season to taste with salt and pepper. Serve over "Potato Gnocchi," sprinkled with parsley.

SERVES 4

SARA KATE'S BAKED GARLIC CHICKEN

In this easy one-dish meal, the potatoes absorb flavor from the garlic and chicken.

2 pounds red potatoes, quartered
1 cup roughly chopped red onion
10 garlic cloves, peeled and halved lengthwise
2 tablespoons chopped fresh rosemary
6 chicken breast halves
salt and pepper

Preheat oven to 400 degrees F. Lightly oil a 13- x 9-inch baking dish.

In a small bowl, combine potatoes, onion, garlic, and rosemary. Layer half of mixture over bottom of prepared baking dish. Arrange chicken on top, and season with salt and pepper to taste. Scatter remaining potato mixture over chicken. Bake uncovered 35 to 45 minutes or until chicken is golden and potatoes are tender.

SERVES 6

CURRIED CRAB
BAKED POTATOES

This fragrant seafood curry served over an open baked potato makes a satisfying, complete meal.

3 tablespoons oil
1 medium onion, chopped
1 teaspoon chopped fresh ginger
2 garlic cloves, chopped
1 teaspoon curry powder
1 cup chicken broth
1 teaspoon Thai fish sauce
1 pound cooked, flaked crabmeat
4 large hot "Quick-as-They're-Gonna-Be
   Baked Potatoes" potatoes (see page 76)

In a large skillet, heat oil over medium-high heat. Sauté onion, ginger, and garlic until onion is soft, about 5 minutes. Add curry powder, and cook 1 minute longer. Add broth and fish sauce. Bring to a boil, and stir in crab. Reduce to a simmer, and cook just until crab is heated through. Serve over open-faced baked potatoes.

SERVES 4

"Clever man that he is, he realized early on that if you give people potatoes, potatoes, and more potatoes, they'll be eternally grateful, forever fulfilled."
—Patricia Wells on Joel Robuchon in Simply French

ROASTED SEABASS
IN POTATO CRUST

In this elegant entrée, crisp potato scallops resemble the scales of a fish.

1 or 2 large baking potatoes, peeled
¼ cup olive oil
salt and pepper
2 garlic cloves, minced
2 cups loosely packed arugula leaves
4 sea bass fillets, about 1½ pounds

Preheat oven to 400 degrees F. Lightly oil a baking sheet.

Using the thin slicing blade of a food processor, the thinnest setting on a mandoline, or a vegetable peeler, slice potatoes lengthwise. Arrange on a prepared baking sheet and lightly brush with oil. Bake about 3 minutes, or just until softened. Sprinkle lightly with salt and pepper and let cool.

In a skillet, heat 1 tablespoon of the oil over

medium-high heat. Sauté garlic 1 minute. Add arugula leaves and stir and cook just until wilted.

Season fish all over with salt and pepper. Divide arugula, and top each piece of fish with a layer of arugula, lightly pressing down.

On each of 4 rectangles of plastic wrap, arrange enough potato slices, slightly overlapping, to create a rectangle large enough to enclose a fish fillet. Set fish at one end of potatoes and, lifting plastic, fold potatoes around fish to enclose. Tightly seal plastic to enclose each potato-wrapped piece of fish. Chill at least 1 hour.

Preheat oven to 400 degrees. In a large skillet, heat remaining oil over high heat. Remove plastic, and add fish to pan. Cook, turning carefully, just until potatoes are golden. Transfer to baking sheet, and roast about 10 minutes to finish cooking the fish.

SERVES 4

SKORDALIA

Mashed garlic combined with potatoes and fragrant olive oil make a wonderful rustic sauce from Greece.

7 garlic cloves
salt
¾ pound baking potato, peeled, cooked, and
    mashed
1 cup extra virgin olive oil
⅓ cup white wine vinegar

In a mortar with a pestle or in a bowl with back of a wooden spoon, mash garlic with 2 teaspoons salt. Add potatoes, and pound with pestle or work with back of spoon until paste is formed. (Do not use food processor or blender.) Gradually beat in olive oil alternately with vinegar until mixture is creamy, adding a little water if necessary. Season to taste with salt. Serve over fish, roasted beets, or eggplant, or as a spread for bread.

MAKES 3 CUPS

A SIDE
OF POTATOES

ROASTED APPLES AND SWEET POTATOES

Marta di Paolo, who is from Colombia, brings this wonderful casserole to Thanksgiving dinners.

2 large sweet potatoes, halved
3 Fuji apples, peeled, cored, cut in large
   chunks
2 tablespoons butter
1 teaspoon brown sugar
½ teaspoon salt
¼ teaspoon cinnamon
⅛ teaspoon allspice

Boil potatoes in enough water to cover for 10 minutes. Let cool, then peel and cut into large chunks.

Preheat oven to 400 degrees F. Coat a 9- x 12-inch baking pan with 1 teaspoon of butter.

Arrange potato and apple chunks in single layer in pan. Combine brown sugar, salt, cinnamon, and allspice. Sprinkle mixture over potatoes and apples. Dot with remaining butter. Bake 45 to 55 minutes, until potatoes are done. Serve hot.

SERVES 4

POTATO PIE

*Here's a terrific make-ahead accompaniment for a
cold-weather dinner.*

1¾ pounds baking potatoes, peeled and
  thinly sliced
2 frozen pie crusts, defrosted
1 small onion, chopped
4 garlic cloves, chopped
1½ teaspoons salt
1 teaspoon pepper
1 cup sour cream
1 egg, lightly beaten
2 tablespoons chopped chives

Cook potatoes in boiling water to cover, for 15 minutes. Drain and set aside.

Preheat oven to 400 degrees F.

Line a 9-inch pie plate with pie crust. Arrange layer of potato slices in bottom of pie. Sprinkle with onion, garlic, salt, and pepper. Continue layering until all potatoes are used.

In small bowl, whisk sour cream, egg, and chives. Pour over potatoes.

Roll out remaining half of dough, and cover pie. Seal and flute edges as desired. Cut several slits in top. Bake 35 minutes. Serve hot.

SERVES 6

You Say "Potato"

In South America, the birthplace of potatoes, they are called "papas." But when they were introduced to England by Sir Walter Raleigh in the sixteenth century, they got the English name "potato" because of their resemblance to another New World tuber: the batata, or sweet potato.

COLCANNON

Colcannon is a traditional Irish side dish of boiled potatoes and cabbage.

2 pounds Yukon gold potatoes, peeled and
   cut into chunks
1 bunch green onions, white and light green
   part only, sliced
1 small head green cabbage, cored and
   roughly chopped
½ cup milk
½ stick butter
salt and pepper

Place potatoes in large pot or Dutch oven. Add cold water just to cover. Arrange onions and cabbage over potatoes. Bring to a boil, then reduce to a simmer, and cook covered until potatoes are tender, about 20 minutes. Drain, then return to low heat, and add milk and butter. Mash with a fork or potato masher.

SERVES 6

TWO-POTATO PANCAKE

This oversized pancake is a great way to get that good fried-potato feeling on the table in a jiffy.

2 baking potatoes, peeled and finely shredded
½ teaspoon salt
freshly ground pepper
¼ cup vegetable oil

Combine potatoes, salt, and pepper in a bowl. Squeeze out excess water, and drain.

Heat 2 tablespoons of the oil in a large nonstick or cast-iron skillet over medium-high heat. Using a spatula, spread the potatoes in a single layer in the pan. Fry until bottom is golden brown, about 7 minutes, and transfer with spatula to platter. Carefully turn over and slide pancake back into pan, crisp-side up. Fry until second side is crisp and golden brown, 7 minutes longer. Slide onto serving platter, and sprinkle with salt.

SERVES 4

POTATO GRUYÈRE GRATIN

Melted cheese and creamy potatoes come together beautifully in this classic French bistro side dish. Serve hot with a winter roast and don't stint on the cream.

butter for coating
1 cup heavy cream
3 garlic cloves, minced
4 large baking potatoes, peeled and thinly sliced
salt and freshly ground pepper
½ teaspoon ground nutmeg
1 cup grated Gruyère cheese

Preheat oven to 350 degrees F. Coat a 9- x 12-inch glass or ceramic roasting pan with butter. In a small saucepan, bring the cream to a boil.

Divide the garlic into 3 parts and sprinkle a third over bottom of the roasting pan. Top with half the potatoes in an even layer. Sprinkle with a third of the garlic, salt, pepper, and nutmeg. Top with remaining potato slices. Pour the hot cream over all. Sprinkle the top with remaining garlic, salt, pepper, and nutmeg. Top with grated cheese. Bake uncovered, about 1 hour, until the top is golden brown and bubbly. Serve hot.

SERVES 4

POTATO LATKES

Use the finest shredding blade of the food processor for these crisp, lacy potato pancakes. Serve with applesauce and sour cream, and do not make too far in advance. Nothing compares to potato pancakes fresh from the frying pan.

4 large baking potatoes, peeled and finely
   shredded
1 medium onion, grated
2 eggs, beaten
3 tablespoons all-purpose flour
1 teaspoon salt
½ teaspoon pepper
corn or peanut oil for frying

In a large bowl, combine potatoes, onion, eggs, flour, salt, and pepper. Mix well with a spoon.

Heat oven to 200 degrees F.

Pour oil to a depth of ¼-inch in 1 or 2 large skillets. Heat over medium-high heat, and spread paper towels nearby. Using 2 spoons, drop the batter by large spoonfuls into hot oil, flattening with the back of a spoon to form 3-inch circles. (The trick to great latke frying is to keep draining excess liquid from potato mixture as it sits.) Fry until golden brown on one side, then flip, and cook the second side until golden brown. Drain on the paper towels. To keep warm, transfer to a baking sheet in single layer. Serve hot with applesauce and sour cream.

MAKES 3 DOZEN LATKES

OVEN-ROASTED POTATO CRISPS

These crisps are a good choice when you crave the flavor of fried potatoes but have no time for frying.

3 large baking potatoes, peeled and thinly sliced
⅓ cup olive oil
salt and freshly ground black pepper

Preheat the oven to 450 degrees F.

Place the potato slices in a large bowl. Rinse under cold running water until the water runs clear, about 5 minutes. Drain and pat dry.

In a large bowl, combine the potatoes and oil with plenty of salt and pepper. Toss to coat. Layer the potatoes, no more than 2 deep and slightly overlapping, in a large jelly roll pan or baking sheet. Bake until the edges are golden brown and crisp, about 30 minutes. Drain any excess oil, and cut into wedges to serve.

SERVES 6

MATCHSTICK FRIES

Nothing beats homemade fries. Prove your devotion to the family, and fry them up a batch.

small baking potatoes, peeled
peanut oil for frying
salt to taste

Using the julienne blade of the food processor or mandolin, cut the potatoes into $\frac{1}{16}$-inch juliennes or matchsticks. Place in a large bowl under cold running water, and rinse until water runs clear. Drain, and pat dry with paper towels.

Pour oil into deep fryer or stockpot, about 5 inches deep. Heat to deep-fry temperature, 350 degrees F. To test oil, toss in one piece. With slotted spoon, transfer to paper towels to drain. Sprinkle with salt, and serve.

WILD MUSHROOM
POTATO GRATIN

This low-fat gratin is a nice accompaniment to an Italian roasted dinner.

olive oil
1 rosemary sprig
3 medium baking potatoes, peeled and thinly
    sliced
½ pound cremini or brown mushrooms,
    cleaned and thinly sliced
3 garlic cloves, thinly sliced
salt and freshly ground pepper

Preheat the oven to 425 degrees F. Coat a 9-inch ovenproof baking dish with olive oil.

Lay the rosemary sprig on the bottom of the dish. Layer half the potatoes on bottom. Top with the mushrooms and half the garlic. Sprinkle generously with olive oil, salt, and pepper.

Top with remaining potatoes and garlic. Sprinkle generously with olive oil, salt, and pepper. Bake uncovered until top is golden and crusty, about 1 hour. Serve hot.

SERVES 4

CLASSIC MASHED POTATOES

The trick to rich, luxurious mashed potatoes is to mash the potatoes while they're still warm and to warm the additions as well.

2 pounds baking potatoes, peeled and
    quartered
salt
½ cup sour cream
4 tablespoons butter
salt and freshly ground pepper

Place potatoes in a medium saucepan, and add enough water to generously cover. Add salt. Bring to a boil, reduce to a simmer, and cook uncovered until soft, 15 to 20 minutes.

Meanwhile combine the sour cream and butter in a small saucepan, and cook over low heat until butter is melted.

Drain the potatoes, and return them to the pot over low heat. Mash by hand with a masher or fork until nearly smooth. Then fold in the warm butter mixture, seasoning with salt and pepper to taste. Serve hot.

SERVES 4 TO 6

ROASTED GARLIC
MASHED POTATOES

When we say garlic potatoes, we mean garlic.
True garlic fiends may even want to pump it up to
eight heads. Delicious!

4 heads garlic, unpeeled, with tops trimmed
olive oil for drizzling
2½ pounds baking potatoes, peeled and
    quartered
salt, to taste
½ stick butter
½ cup milk
freshly ground pepper, to taste

Preheat the oven to 500 degrees F. Stand the garlic in an olive oil-coated roasting pan. Drizzle the tops with more oil. Bake uncovered until soft, about 25 minutes. Let cool, then separate the cloves and press each with your fingers to peel. Mash the pulp with a fork.

Boil the potatoes in a medium saucepan of salted water until tender, about 20 minutes.

Meanwhile combine the mashed garlic, butter, milk, salt, and pepper in a small saucepan. Cook over low heat, stirring occasionally, until the butter is melted.

Drain the cooked potatoes, and mash in the pot with a fork or potato masher. Return to low heat. Add the garlic mixture, and mash until well combined. Season generously with salt and pepper, and add more butter to taste. Serve hot.

SERVES 4

MASHED YAMS WITH LIME AND HONEY

Chefs Mary Sue Milliken and Susan Feniger of Border Grill fame taught me this great side dish for the winter holiday table.

3 large yams, unpeeled
3 tablespoons butter, room temperature
¼ cup sour cream
3 tablespoons lime juice
salt and freshly ground pepper
1 tablespoon honey, or more to taste

Preheat the oven to 350 degrees F. Bake the yams on a baking tray in the oven until puffy and oozing, about 1½ hours. Set yams aside to cool slightly, leaving the oven on.

When cool enough to handle, peel the yams and place in a medium baking dish. Add the butter, sour cream, lime juice, salt, pepper, and honey. Mash well to combine, drizzling more honey on top if desired. Return to the oven, and bake until heated through. Serve hot.

SERVES 6

SMASHED POTATOES
WITH BLACK OLIVES

These chunky, golden mashed potatoes, inspired by the French chef Roger Verge, are rich with flavor—not fat.

1 pound Yukon gold potatoes, cut in large
    chunks
1 tablespoon salt, or more to taste
½ cup extra virgin olive oil
2 garlic cloves, crushed and peeled
½ cup Niçoise or Kalamata olives, pitted and
    roughly chopped
freshly ground pepper

Place the potatoes in a medium saucepan, and cover generously with cold water. Add salt. Bring to a boil, reduce to a simmer, and cook uncovered until potatoes are done, 20 to 30 minutes depending on size. Drain and cool slightly.

Meanwhile heat the olive oil with garlic in a small saucepan over low heat until garlic turns golden. Remove and discard garlic.

Holding the hot potatoes in a towel, slip off the skins with a knife. Return the potatoes to the pot, and roughly mash with a fork. Place over very low heat and drizzle in hot oil, mashing and mixing with a fork. Add olives, salt and pepper to taste, and mash to combine, leaving lumps to taste. Serve hot.

SERVES 4

QUICK-AS-THEY'RE-GONNA-BE BAKED POTATOES

Baked potatoes should come out perfect every time with this foolproof method. For old-school stalwarts, the conventional oven method is included.

■ Idaho, russets, or baking potatoes

Scrub the potatoes under cold running water to remove dirt, and pat dry. Trim and discard any eyes.

In the microwave: With a skewer or fork, puncture potatoes a few times all over. Loosely wrap each in a plain paper towel and follow your microwave's directions: about 5 minutes at high power for one potato; 8 minutes for two; 14 minutes for four. Carefully remove and let sit, wrapped in a towel, 5 minutes to finish cooking.

In the oven: Bake on rack in preheated 425 degrees F oven for 1 hour. Do not wrap in foil. For crisp skin, rub with soft butter before baking.

STEAMED ROASTERS

Roasting potatoes with a little bit of water accentuates their creaminess without adding much fat.

3 pounds boiling potatoes, with skins
4 garlic cloves, peeled and crushed
2 small sprigs rosemary or thyme
¼ cup olive oil
salt and freshly ground pepper
¼ cup cold water

Preheat oven to 400 degrees F.

Cut large potatoes into quarters; leave small ones whole. Place in a large bowl with garlic, herb sprigs, oil, salt and pepper. Toss to combine. Arrange in a single layer in a large roasting pan. Drizzle with water and cover tightly with foil.

Bake 1 hour, or until tender. Remove the foil, and return the pan to the oven 5 to 10 minutes to brown slightly.

SERVES 6

CHIPOTLE-STUFFED
BAKED POTATOES

4 baking potatoes
1 chipotle chile, toasted and soaked in hot
    water 20 minutes
2 tablespoons butter
1 teaspoon ground cumin
½ cup sour cream
2 teaspoons honey
2 tablespoons chopped fresh cilantro
salt and freshly ground pepper, to taste
2 tablespoons grated Parmesan cheese
4 thinly sliced scallions (optional)

Preheat oven to 400 degrees F. Wash the potatoes, and place on oven rack to bake, 1 hour. Transfer to baking sheet and cool 5 minutes, leaving oven on.

Meanwhile remove the seeds and stem from soaked chipotle, and mince the flesh. Melt the butter in a small skillet over low heat. Add the cumin and chipotle, and cook, shaking the pan occasionally, until fragrant, about 3 minutes. Transfer to a medium bowl, add the sour cream and honey, and blend.

Halve each hot potato lengthwise. With a spoon, scoop out the flesh, leaving a ½-inch-thick shell. Transfer flesh to a bowl with sour cream mixture and mash and blend until smooth. Mash in cilantro, salt, and pepper. Spoon potato mixture back into skins, mounding slightly, and then sprinkle the tops with Parmesan. Place on a baking sheet, and bake 30 minutes, until golden. Sprinkle with scallions, if desired, and serve hot.

SERVES 4

BLUE CHEESE-BACON BAKED POTATOES

4 baking potatoes
⅔ cup crumbled blue cheese
3 slices fried bacon, crumbled
½ cup sour cream
salt and freshly ground pepper, to taste
2 tablespoons butter
2 tablespoons grated Parmesan cheese
4 scallions, thinly sliced, for garnish

Preheat the oven to 400 degrees F. Wash the potatoes, and place on oven rack to bake for 1 hour. Transfer to baking sheet and cool 5 minutes, leaving oven on.

In a large mixing bowl, mix together blue cheese, bacon, sour cream, salt, and pepper. Set aside.

Halve each hot potato lengthwise. With a spoon, scoop out the flesh, leaving a ¼-inch-thick shell. Transfer flesh to the bowl with the sour cream mixture, and mash and blend until smooth. Spoon potato mixture back into skins, mounding slightly. Dot the tops with butter, and sprinkle with Parmesan. Place on baking sheet, and bake 30 minutes, until golden. Sprinkle with scallions, and serve hot.

SERVES 4

BOILED NEW POTATOES WITH PARSLEY AND BUTTER

This simple treatment for small new potatoes is the perfect accompaniment to a well-cooked piece of fish.

small new red or white boiling potatoes
butter
salt and freshly ground pepper

Place the potatoes in a saucepan, and add cold water to generously cover. Salt the water, and bring to a boil. Cook at a low boil, uncovered, 20 to 25 minutes. To test for doneness, pierce a potato with a knife or fork. It should plunge in without resistance. Drain and return to the pot.

Place the pot over low heat, add butter, salt, and pepper to taste, and partially cover. Cook, shaking the pan occasionally, 5 minutes longer. Serve hot, with the butter from the pan.

SALT-ROASTED POTATOES

Good potatoes won't even need any butter after this elegant treatment.

1 box coarse kosher salt
Yukon golds, yellow Finns, or any small boiling
   potatoes

Preheat oven to 450 degrees F.

Pour salt, 1 inch deep, into glass or ceramic roasting pan large enough to hold potatoes. Tuck potatoes into salt and then pour on additional salt, enough to entirely cover potatoes. Bake uncovered 1 hour. Cool slightly, lift out potatoes, and brush off salt. Serve hot with salt and pepper, or use in salads.

PAN-FRIED POTATOES WITH PEPPERS AND ONIONS

You can serve this hash of fried vegetables along-side breakfast eggs or any grilled meat.

2 baking potatoes, peeled
1 medium onion
1 medium red bell pepper
1 medium green pepper
6 tablespoons vegetable oil
1 garlic clove, chopped
salt and freshly ground pepper
3 tablespoons chopped fresh herbs such as
   basil, parsley, oregano, marjoram

Cut the potatoes, onion, and peppers into ½-inch dice.

Heat ¼ cup oil in a large nonstick skillet over high heat. Pat the potatoes dry and fry about 20 minutes, turning until golden all over. Remove with slotted spoon, and drain on paper towels.

Reduce the heat to medium, and sauté the onion and garlic with salt and pepper, about 3 minutes. Add peppers, and continue cooking until peppers soften and onions brown, about 15 minutes. Salt the potatoes, add them to the pan along with the herbs, and stir and toss to combine. Cook just to heat through and blend the flavors, about 4 minutes. Serve hot.

SERVES 4

SAUTÉED POTATOES

These double-cooked potatoes are elegant and easy to do on the stovetop while a roast crackles in the oven.

1 pound boiling potatoes, with skins
1 tablespoon salt
3 tablespoons butter or more to taste
salt and freshly ground pepper, to taste
paprika, to taste
2 tablespoons chopped fresh parsley

Place the potatoes in a saucepan, and generously cover with cold water. Add about a tablespoon of salt, and bring to a boil. Reduce to a simmer, and cook just until tender, 15 to 25 minutes. Drain and return to pot. Place over low heat, and cook 2 or 3 minutes, shaking the pan, to dry the potatoes. Let cool.

Peel the potatoes, and cut into ¼-inch slices lengthwise. In a nonstick skillet, melt 2 tablespoons of the butter over medium heat. Sauté the slices in a single layer until golden on both sides, about 10 minutes total. Add the remaining butter or more, to taste, if the pan is dry. Season with salt, pepper, paprika, and parsley, and serve hot.

SERVES 2 TO 4

POTATOES ANNA

Indulge in this wonderful rich cake of layered potatoes and butter for a special occasion dinner.

1 stick butter
1½ pounds baking potatoes, peeled and thinly
    sliced
salt and pepper

Preheat oven to 400 degrees F.

In a small ovenproof skillet over medium heat, melt half the butter, tipping pan to coat bottom and sides evenly. Remove from heat, and arrange potato slices in overlapping concentric circles. Add remaining potato slices in layers, dotting each layer with remaining butter, and seasoning lightly with salt and pepper. Place over medium heat until potatoes are browned on bottom, 10 to 15 minutes.

Transfer to oven, and bake 25 minutes. To serve, loosen edges and invert onto plate.

SERVES 4

THE POTATO
BAKERY

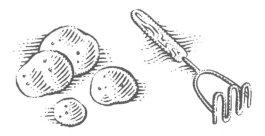

CHOCOLATE POTATO CAKE

Potatoes add an extra dollop of richness to this moist chocolate layer cake.

½ cup milk
4 ounces unsweetened chocolate
1½ cups hot "Classic Mashed Potatoes" (see page 68)
2 cups cake flour
1 tablespoon baking powder
¼ teaspoon salt
2 sticks butter, room temperature
2 cups sugar
4 eggs, separated
1½ teaspoons vanilla
prepared chocolate frosting

Preheat oven to 350 degrees F. Line two 9-inch round cake pans with waxed paper. Butter the paper.

In the top of a double boiler set over simmering water, heat milk and chocolate, stirring constantly, until chocolate is melted. Remove from heat and stir in mashed potato. Blend well.

Sift flour, baking powder, and salt into a bowl.

In a large mixing bowl, cream butter and 1¼ cups sugar until light. Blend in chocolate mixture. Then add egg yolks and vanilla, and beat to blend. Gradually stir in dry ingredients.

In another bowl, with clean beaters, whisk egg whites until stiff. Gradually beat in remaining sugar. Fold egg whites into batter. Pour into prepared pans, and bake 30 minutes or until cake springs back when pressed in center.

Cool on rack 10 minutes, then turn out onto rack and cool completely. Spread frosting between layers, and on top and sides.

SERVES 12

SWEET POTATO PIE

If you've never made this classic Southern dessert, you'll be happily surprised at how easy it is to make.

1 frozen pie crust, defrosted
1 large sweet potato, baked and cooled
4 tablespoons butter
2 eggs
2 egg yolks
½ cup brown sugar
¾ cup dark corn syrup
1 tablespoon vanilla
¼ teaspoon allspice

Roll out crust to line a 10-inch tart or pie pan. Chill crust in pan ½ hour.

Preheat oven to 375 degrees F.

When potato is cool, peel and cut into ½-inch cubes.

Line tart shell with foil, prick with a fork, and fill with weights. Bake 10 minutes. Remove from oven, and remove weights.

Melt the butter in a small pan over low heat until browned bits are on bottom. Remove from heat.

In a large bowl, beat together eggs, yolks, brown sugar, corn syrup, vanilla, and allspice until smooth. Stir in melted butter. Spread the potato cubes in bottom crust. Pour in filling, and bake ½ hour, until tester inserted in center comes out clean. Cool on rack.

MAKES 1 PIE

POTATO BREAD

This crusty yellow loaf gets its extra moistness from a mashed potato in the dough. It's great for toasting or sandwich making.

1 baking potato, peeled and cut in chunks
1 cup low-fat milk
3 tablespoons softened butter
1 teaspoon salt
1 tablespoon sugar
1 package dry yeast
⅓ cup warm water
5 cups bread flour
1 egg white beaten with 1 tablespoon water,
    for egg wash

Place the potato in a pot with enough water to cover. Boil until soft, 20 minutes. Drain, reserving cooking water, and mash the potato in a bowl.

Scald milk and combine with ½ cup reserved cooking liquid. Place in the bowl of an electric mixer. Add potato, butter, salt, and sugar. Cool to room temperature.

In a small bowl, combine yeast and warm water, and set aside 10 minutes. When milk mixture has cooled, pour in yeast. Add flour, and knead with dough hook on low speed about 8 minutes, until smooth.

Transfer to a buttered bowl, cover with a towel, and set aside to rise, about ½ hour. On a counter, punch down dough and briefly knead. Divide dough in half and transfer to two buttered loaf pans. Cover and let rise until doubled, about 45 minutes.

Preheat oven to 350 degrees F.

Brush the tops of loaves with egg wash. Bake about 1 hour, until tops are golden and bread sounds hollow when tapped. Turn out, and cool on a rack.

MAKES 2 LOAVES

POTATO PIE CRUST

Use this rustic crust for potpies or other savory pies.

1½ cups all-purpose flour
1 teaspoon salt
1 cup mashed baking potato, chilled
1 stick butter, cut in small pieces, chilled
2 tablespoons ice water

In a bowl, combine flour, salt, and sugar. Add potato, and mix well. Blend in butter with your fingertips or a pastry blender until mixture looks like coarse meal. Mix in water with a fork.

Turn dough out onto work surface, and knead into a ball. Wrap in plastic and chill at least 1 hour. Pie dough can be stored in the refrigerator up to 4 days or in freezer 1 month.

MAKES TWO 9-INCH CRUSTS